921
KEN

Smith, Kathie Bil-
lingslea

John F. Kennedy

DATE DUE

BRODART	08/90	7.98

THE GREAT AMERICANS SERIES

John F. Kennedy

By Kathie Billingslea Smith

Illustrated by James Seward

Julian Messner
New York

Cover Portrait: Sam Patrick

Library of Congress Cataloging-in-Publication Data

Smith, Kathie Billingslea.
  John F. Kennedy.

  (Great Americans)
  Julian Messner
  1. Kennedy, John F. (John Fitzgerald), 1917–1963—
Juvenile literature. 2. Presidents—United States—
Biography—Juvenile literature. I. Title.
II. Series: Great Americans (New York, N.Y.)
E842.Z9S63 1987 973.922'092'4 [B] 86-33863
ISBN 0-671-64602-8

John Fitzgerald Kennedy was the thirty-fifth President of the United States. Although he served for less than three years, he is remembered by many as a brave, caring man and a dynamic leader.

John F. Kennedy was born on May 29, 1917, into a Massachusetts family known for its wealth and interest in politics. His father, Joseph Kennedy, was a multi-millionaire businessman, and his grandfather, John Fitzgerald, had been the mayor of Boston. John, or "Jack" as he was known, was the second of nine children born to Joseph and Rose Kennedy.

The Kennedys were an active family who loved to compete with one another in sports and other events.

"Come in a winner," Joe Kennedy told his children. "Second place is no good."

Jack was a thin, sickly child. Forced to spend long periods of time in bed, he developed a love of reading.

Jack was not a strong athlete or a good student like his older brother Joe, Jr. They both attended Choate, a boarding school in Connecticut. It was difficult for Jack to follow behind his successful older brother. But Jack was very popular in school and had lots of friends. He was still an avid reader—the only fourteen-year-old at school who subscribed to The New York Times and read it from cover to cover each morning.

The Kennedy family spent summers at their seaside home in Hyannis Port, Massachusetts. Jack had his own sailboat and was an excellent sailor and swimmer. He loved the sea.

In the fall of 1936, after losing a year of school due to sickness, Jack enrolled at Harvard University. He hurt his back playing freshman football. This injury would plague him for the rest of his life.

After his father was appointed to be the U.S. Ambassador to Great Britain, Jack took some time off from school to travel and study the situation in Europe. It looked as if another World War would soon begin. Jack became very interested in world affairs and gave his father reports on the fighting.

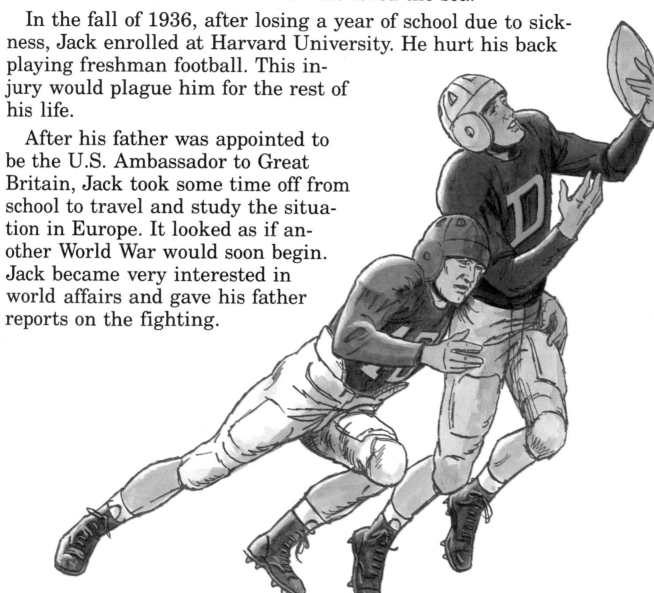

Jack returned to Harvard with a new interest in learning. He began to do very well in his studies. One of his research papers won awards. Later it was rewritten and published as a best-selling book.

After graduation, Jack tried to enlist in the army, but was told that his back injury disqualified him from serving in the military. Jack worked for five months to strengthen his back and joined the Navy in September.

On December 7, 1941, the Japanese bombed Pearl Harbor, and the United States immediately entered World War II.

Joe, Jr., a trained pilot, was stationed in England.

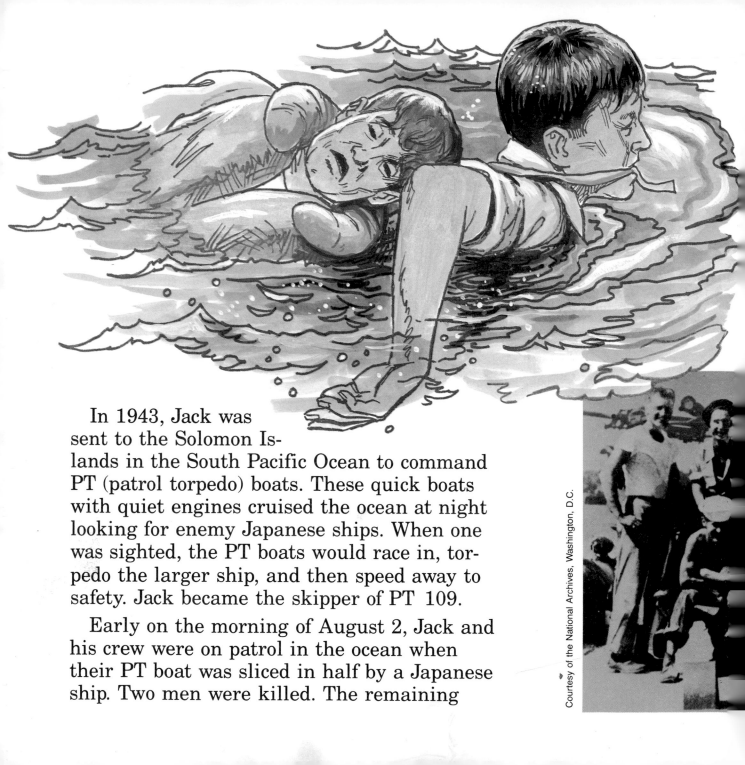

In 1943, Jack was sent to the Solomon Islands in the South Pacific Ocean to command PT (patrol torpedo) boats. These quick boats with quiet engines cruised the ocean at night looking for enemy Japanese ships. When one was sighted, the PT boats would race in, torpedo the larger ship, and then speed away to safety. Jack became the skipper of PT 109.

Early on the morning of August 2, Jack and his crew were on patrol in the ocean when their PT boat was sliced in half by a Japanese ship. Two men were killed. The remaining eleven managed to swim four miles through open seas to the closest island. Jack towed a burned crewmate by holding the man's life jacket strap in his teeth as he swam.

For seven days Jack and his crew hid from the Japanese by day and swam from island to island at night, hoping to get rescued. Jack met two friendly natives traveling in a canoe. They could not speak English but carried a message to the American troops 38 miles away. Jack carved the message on a piece of coconut. It read:

NATIVE KNOWS POSIT
HE CAN PILOT   11 ALIVE NEED
SMALL BOAT   KENNEDY

Soon after that, the sailors were rescued. Jack Kennedy was awarded the Purple Heart, and Navy and Marine Medal for his brave actions. Seventeen years later when he became President of the United States, Jack kept the coconut with the carved message on top of his desk at the White House.

◄ Lt. Comd. Kennedy (extreme right) and the crew of the PT 109.

In November of 1943, Jack returned home. He was sick with malaria and had severe back problems. While he was recuperating from a back operation, his family received word that Joe, Jr. had been killed when his bomber plane exploded in mid-air. The family was grief-stricken. Jack's father, who had had great plans for Joe, Jr.'s future in politics, now placed all his hopes upon Jack.

In 1946, Jack campaigned to be elected a member of the House of Representatives from Massachusetts. His whole family became involved in his campaign. As a rich, young war hero, Jack captured people's attention. He easily won the election.

Jack moved to Washington, D.C. With his boyish looks and thin frame, he hardly looked old enough to be a U.S. Congressman. But he quickly became known for handling problems easily and well.

In May of 1948, tragedy once again struck the Kennedy family. Jack's favorite sister, Kathleen, was killed in a plane crash in France. Jack grieved privately, but kept up a busy schedule of weekdays spent working in Washington and weekends spent speaking and traveling in Massachusetts. In November, he was re-elected to his second term in the House of Representatives.

Jack's back pains were now much worse. He often had to walk with crutches. When he gave a speech, however, he left the crutches in his car and walked alone, smiling broadly and giving no sign of the intense pain he felt. Several times during the day he would find a hot tub in which to soak his aching back. Never one to waste a minute, he used these times to read books and discuss problems with his

closest advisors. These "tub talks" were a regular part of his schedule for the rest of his life.

In 1952, Kennedy began a new campaign to become a U.S. Senator from Massachusetts. His twenty-seven-year-old brother, Bobby, served as his campaign manager. Jack ran against the current senator Henry Cabot Lodge. At first Jack was viewed as an underdog, but his friendly personality and hard work won the hearts of many voters. Lodge himself later remarked that Kennedy was "an extraordinarily likable man. In fact, I liked him," he added.

Jack won the election by a narrow margin and was sworn into office on January 3, 1953.

Back in Washington, D.C., Jack began dating Jacqueline Lee Bouvier, a photographer for a Washington newspaper. In May 1953, she flew to England to cover the coronation of Queen Elizabeth II. Jack was waiting at the airport when she returned home and proposed to her as she stepped off the plane. They were married in Newport, Rhode Island, on September 12, 1953. Thousands of people lined up outside the church to see the popular senator and his new wife.

After a honeymoon in Mexico, Jack and Jackie returned to Washington and a busy schedule of meetings, banquets, and speeches.

Before long Jack's back pain became unbearable. He had two more operations and almost died. Jackie provided constant support. Throughout the ordeal, Jack seldom complained.

"Everyone admires courage," he often said, "and the greenest garlands are for those who possess it."

While Jack was in the hospital, he wrote a book of stories about people who had shown great bravery in life. The book, <u>Profiles in Courage,</u> was later awarded a Pulitzer Prize for fine writing.

By March 1955, Jack was able to walk without crutches, and by May he was back at work in Washington. Doctors told him that he would never be completely free from pain and fitted him with a back brace to be worn every day.

◄ The Capitol in Washington, D.C.

Jack, Jackie and Caroline. ▶

On November 27, 1957, Jackie gave birth to a baby daughter named Caroline. Jack was thrilled to be a father.

In 1958 he easily won re-election to his Senate seat and established himself as one of the best-known Democrats in the nation. The next year, he decided to run for the office of President of the United States. Again his whole family gathered to help him campaign. At the Democratic National Convention in 1960, Kennedy was chosen to be the Democratic Presidential candidate.

As he accepted the nomination, he said, ". . . we stand today on the edge of a New Frontier . . . Give me your help . . . Give me your hand . . . your voice and your vote."

The theme of a "New Frontier" became Kennedy's campaign slogan. He spoke of the need for Americans to be more responsible citizens.

Kennedy picked Texas Senator Lyndon Baines Johnson to be his Vice-Presidential running mate. He was the Senate Majority Leader and a popular southern senator.

The Republican Party nominated Richard Nixon, who had been Vice-President under President Eisenhower, as its Presidential candidate, and Henry Cabot Lodge as his running mate.

Kennedy campaigned in 237 cities all over the country. His days were spent meeting people, giving speeches and shaking hands. Seventy million Americans watched as Kennedy and Nixon debated each other on television. With each debate, Kennedy's popularity grew.

Courtesy of the National Archives, Washington, D.C.

On October 19, 1960, Martin Luther King, Jr., a spokesman for equal rights for blacks and whites, was arrested and jailed for quietly refusing to leave a segregated restaurant in Atlanta. Kennedy heard the news and called King's wife to pledge his support and offer his help. King was released from jail the next day. His father, a well-known Baptist minister, said, "I've got a suitcase of votes, and I'm going to take them to Mr. Kennedy, and I'm going to dump them in his lap."

Blacks across the nation rallied in support of Kennedy.

On November 8, 1960, Kennedy was elected President of the United States. The election was a very close one, with Kennedy receiving only 112,881 more votes than Nixon. But Jack Kennedy had "come in a winner."

President John F. Kennedy ▶

President Kennedy talking with Ambassador Dean. ▶

Courtesy of the National Archives, Washington, D.C.

Later that month, a baby son, John F. Kennedy, Jr. was born.

On January 20,1961, Kennedy was inaugurated as the thirty-fifth President of the United States. He challenged Americans to "Ask not what your country can do for you . . . Ask what you can do for your country."

Once in office, Kennedy followed that up by creating the Peace Corps—an organization that sent trained Americans to help people in poorer countries. Thousands of Americans applied to serve.

Kennedy was an energetic President who symbolized youth and vigor (or "vi-gah", as he pronounced it with his Boston accent). He could speed-read 1,200 to 2,000 words per minute and read five newspapers each morning at breakfast. He was often seen dictating a letter to a secretary while holding a different conversation with another person.

The atmosphere at the White House was relaxed and comfortable. For the first time in many years, young children lived there. At age three, Caroline charmed news reporters who asked what her daddy was doing.

"Oh, he's upstairs with his shoes and socks off, doing nothing," she answered.

Fidel Castro ▶

Jackie Kennedy held fine concerts, ballets, and poetry readings at the White House to help Americans experience the best of different cultures. She also began to redecorate the White House with beautiful antique furniture.

In April of 1961, the United States, under President Kennedy's direction, helped a group of Cubans try to overthrow Cuba's Communist leader, Fidel Castro. An invasion was launched at a place called the Bay of Pigs. The attack failed, and the U.S. was criticized for masterminding the plan. Kennedy realized that he had made a serious mistake. But his problems with Cuba were not over.

▲ The President and First Lady talking with Queen Elizabeth and Prince Phillip.

In the Fall of 1962, Kennedy learned that Russian-made missiles were being installed on nearby Cuba. If the missiles were fired, it was estimated that they could kill eighty-million Americans. Kennedy ordered a quarantine of Cuba. He had the U.S. Navy patrol around the island and search all in-coming ships for weapons. Kennedy then demanded that Russian Premier Khrushchev remove the missiles from the island. Khrushchev agreed, and the crisis passed.

The next summer, Jackie gave birth to another son, Patrick. But the baby had difficulty breathing and died soon after birth. This was a sad time for them all.

Courtesy of the National Archives, Washington, D.C.

Nikita Khrushchev ▶

Kennedy believed that all U.S. citizens—black or white or red or yellow—should have the same freedoms listed in the Constitution. But some blacks were not treated fairly in many parts of the country. On June 19, 1963, Kennedy sent a civil rights bill to Congress.

Two months later, he met with Martin Luther King, Jr. at the White House after his famous "I have a dream" speech. Kennedy greeted King and said, "I have a dream—the same dream."

With another Presidential election a year away, Kennedy decided to begin some early campaigning, especially in the southern states where some people were unhappy with his support for civil rights.

Kennedy with
Martin Luther King, Jr. ▶

On November 22, 1963, the Kennedys flew to Texas. Seated in a car with Texas Governor John Connally and his wife, Jack and Jackie rode in a parade through Dallas. Vice-President Johnson and his wife rode in a car behind them. Because it was a sunny day, Kennedy asked that his car's bulletproof bubble top be put down. As the motorcade passed a tall building, rifle shots cracked the air. President Kennedy collapsed onto Jackie. He had bullet wounds in his back and the back of his head.

Secret Service agents jumped on the car to shield the President from further shots, and the car raced to nearby Parkland Memorial Hospital.

At the hospital, doctors worked frantically to save Kennedy's life, but it was too late. John Fitzgerald Kennedy was dead at the age of forty-six. He had only been President for about 1,000 days.

Kennedy's body was placed in a casket and put on board the Presidential jet Air Force One to be taken back to Washington, D.C. Before take-off, Lyndon Baines Johnson was sworn in as the new President of the United States.

Lee Harvey Oswald was arrested for the assassination of President Kennedy. But he never came to trial. Two days later as he was being transferred to a different jail, Oswald was shot and killed by a man named Jack Ruby.

People all over the world were shocked by Kennedy's tragic death. His bronze casket was placed in the rotunda of the Capitol in Washington, D.C. where, almost 100 years before, Abraham Lincoln had lain in state after his assassination. More than 250,000 people walked past in silent tribute.

Kennedy's casket was carried down Pennsylvania Avenue. It was followed by an officer leading a black riderless horse with empty boots reversed in the stirrups. This symbolized the man who would never again ride the horse.

Kennedy was buried near other American soldiers in Arlington Cemetery in Virginia. Near his grave, Jackie lit an eternal flame that still burns there, and always will, providing a small light in memory of a great man.